CLASSICAL THEMES FOR TWO

Arrangements by Peter Deneff

ISBN 978-1-5400-1414-6

7777 W. BLUEMOUND RD. P.O. BOX 13819 MILWAUKEE, WI 53213

In Australia Contact:
Hal Leonard Australia Pty. Ltd.
4 Lentara Court
Cheltenham, Victoria, 3192 Australia
Email: ausadmin@halleonard.com.au

Visit Hal Leonard Online at
www.halleonard.com

ACADEMIC FESTIVAL OVERTURE

TRUMPETS

By JOHANNES BRAHMS

AIR
from WATER MUSIC

TRUMPETS

By GEORGE FRIDERIC HANDEL

Andante con moto

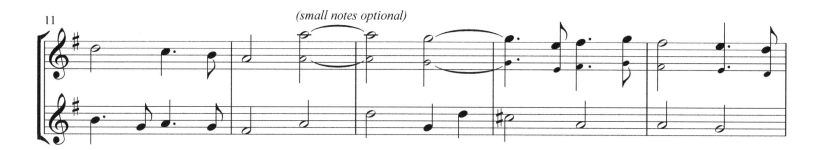

(small notes optional)

To Coda

5

CODA

D.C. al Coda

AIR ON THE G STRING
from ORCHESTRAL SUITE NO. 3 IN D MAJOR, BWV 1068

TRUMPETS

By JOHANN SEBASTIAN BACH

BLUE DANUBE WALTZ

TRUMPETS

By JOHANN STRAUSS, JR.

Moderately

CANON IN D

TRUMPETS

By JOHANN PACHELBEL

CLAIR DE LUNE
from SUITE BERGAMASQUE

TRUMPETS

By CLAUDE DEBUSSY

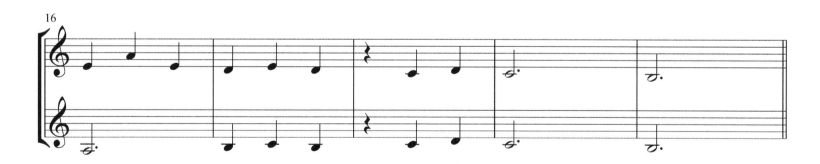

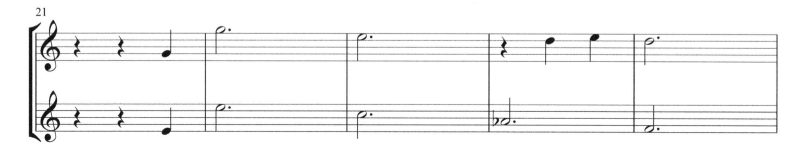

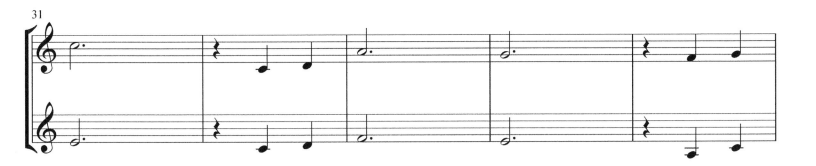

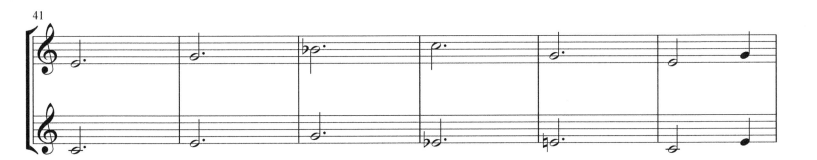

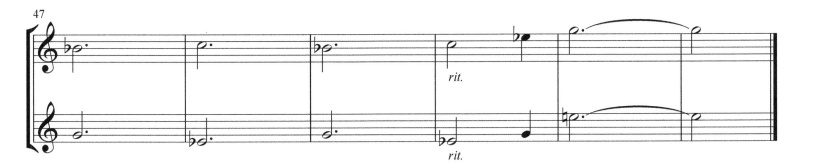

EINE KLEINE NACHTMUSIK
(Second Movement Theme: "Romance")

TRUMPETS

By WOLFGANG AMADEUS MOZART

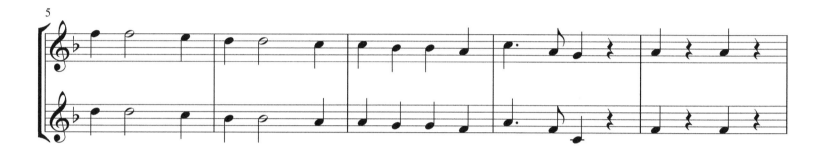

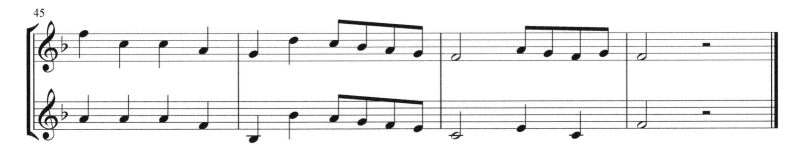

FLOWER DUET
from LAKMÉ

TRUMPETS

By LÉO DELIBES

Andante con moto

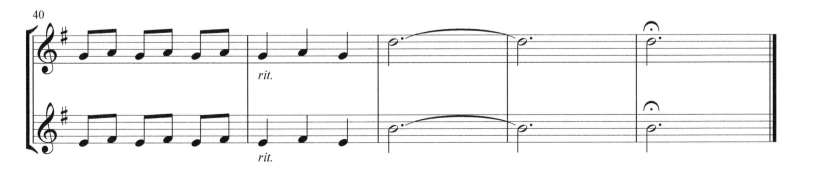

HALLELUJAH CHORUS
from MESSIAH

TRUMPETS

By GEORGE FRIDERIC HANDEL

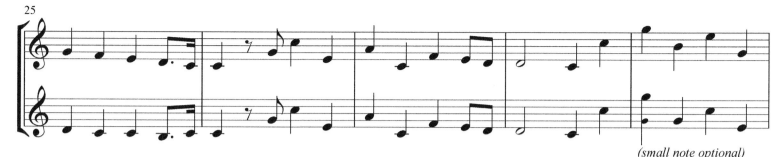

(small note optional)

rit.

rit.

HORNPIPE
from WATER MUSIC

TRUMPETS

By GEORGE FRIDERIC HANDEL

Allegro maestoso

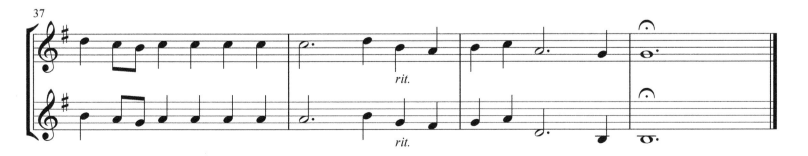

HUNGARIAN DANCE NO. 5

TRUMPETS

By JOHANNES BRAHMS

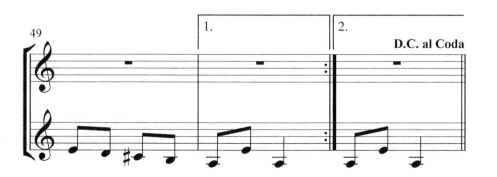

JESU, JOY OF MAN'S DESIRING
from CANTATA 147

TRUMPETS

By JOHANN SEBASTIAN BACH

D.C. al Coda

CODA

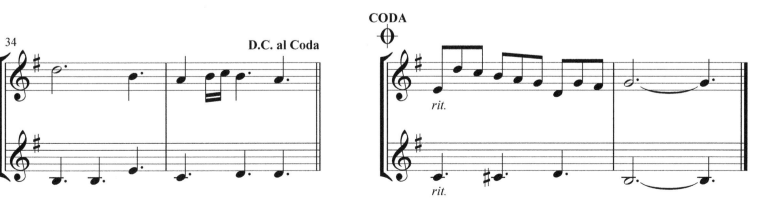

rit.

MARCH
from THE NUTCRACKER

TRUMPETS

By PYOTR IL'YICH TCHAIKOVSKY

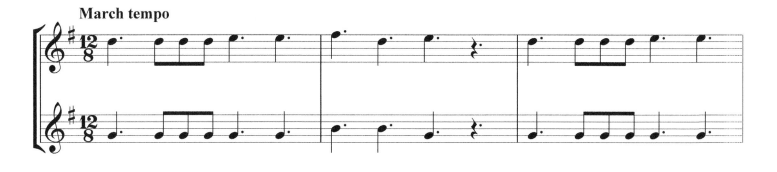

MINUET IN G
from ANNA MAGDALENA NOTEBOOK

By CHRISTIAN PETZOLD
formerly attributed to J.S. Bach

TRUMPETS

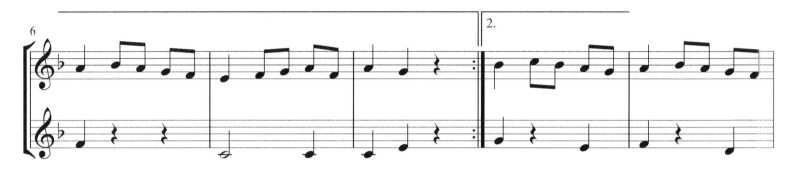

ODE TO JOY
from SYMPHONY NO. 9 IN D MINOR

TRUMPETS

By LUDWIG VAN BEETHOVEN

Allegro

MORNING
from PEER GYNT

TRUMPETS

By EDVARD GRIEG

Allegretto pastorale

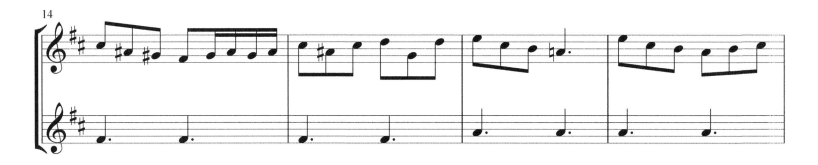

PICTURES AT AN EXHIBITION
(Promenade)

TRUMPETS

By MODEST MUSSORGSKY

POMP AND CIRCUMSTANCE
March No. 1

TRUMPETS

By EDWARD ELGAR

Allegro

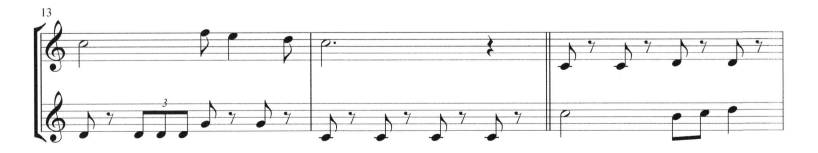

RONDEAU
from SUITE DE SYMPHONIE

By JEAN-JOSEPH MOURET

TRUMPETS

SHEEP MAY SAFELY GRAZE

from CANTATA 208

TRUMPETS

By JOHANN SEBASTIAN BACH

THE SURPRISE SYMPHONY
(Symphony No. 94, Second Movement Theme)

TRUMPETS

By FRANZ JOSEPH HAYDN

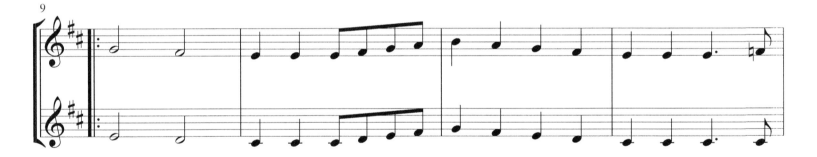

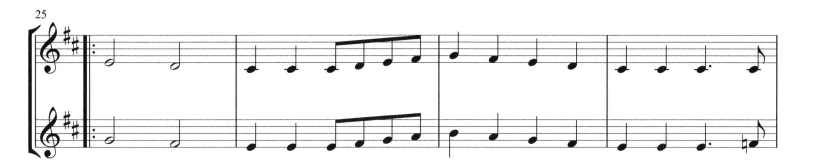

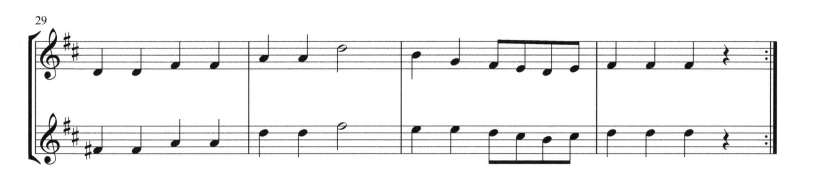

SYMPHONY NO. 7
(Second Movement Theme)

TRUMPETS

By LUDWIG VAN BEETHOVEN

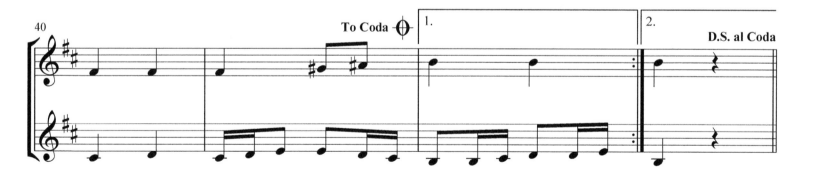

TRUMPET VOLUNTARY
(Prince of Denmark's March)

TRUMPETS

By JEREMIAH CLARKE

WILLIAM TELL OVERTURE
(Theme)

TRUMPETS

By GIOACHINO ROSSINI

Allegro vivace

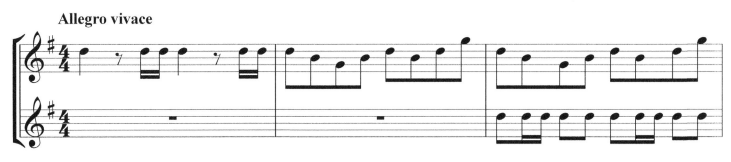